The Trust Is Gone. Help!

The Marriage Rocks Self-Help Guide To
Rebuild Trust In Your Marriage

Davida Grant Brown

ISBN:1508438323

ISBN-13:9781508438328

DEDICATION

I dedicate this book to my husband, Derrick. Your support and encouragement has touched me more than you can imagine. You are truly my other half. I am better because of you.

CONTENTS

ACKNOWLEDGMENTS

I want to thank my family for your support and encouragement. There is no me without you.

INTRODUCTION

I'm so excited that you purchased this workbook. It says that you are open to and hopefully want to move forward in your marriage. You just may not know how to do that, how to get to that happy place again. Well, we're going to share our process and steps to do that in this self-help guide. When you finish this book, you will have the key steps you need to rebuild and restore trust in your marriage.

Before we begin, I want to share a little bit about Marriage Rocks and why I am so passionate about the issue of Trust in marriage. Marriage Rocks is a company dedicated to equipping couples with the tools they need to have a marriage that not only works, but thrives. We educate couples on the key principles to having a successful marriage, and help couples to develop practical skills and implement specific steps to maximize the potential in their marriage.

Marriage Rocks was birthed out of my frustration with what I was seeing in the media. The portrayal of marriage was negative and disheartening. Divorce statistics were seemingly mentioned on the news every day. As for television shows and movies, it seemed as if every major lead was in an adulterous affair or pursuing a married individual. I couldn't take it. I shared my frustration with my husband and we decided to start Marriage Rocks.

Through Marriage Rocks, we want to tell a different story about marriage. We want to shed some positive light on this institution by showing the world that married, committed, and happy couples exist. Marriage is not perfect. It certainly will have its ups and downs. But there are thousands, if not millions, of couples around the world who are putting in the necessary work, and as a result have marriages that thrive. Our mission is, in part, to flood society with positive messages of marriage to help change negative perceptions of marriage. We do this primarily through our online platform, www.yesmarriagerocks.com. There, we showcase couples from all around the world who are proud to say that they have marriages that ROCK. Importantly, these couples share their tips for having a successful marriage. Our hope is that these stories and tips can encourage and inspire other couples to do the same.

Additionally, as I mentioned earlier, Marriage Rocks is also dedicated to helping couples in need so that they too can have a thriving marriage. Because we are so passionate about marriage, my husband Derrick and I immersed ourselves in the study of marriage from a biblical perspective. We are certified marriage coaches through the American Association of Christian Counselors and provide private coaching and webinars on various marital issues. Derrick and I believe that your marriage is the most important investment decision you'll ever make, so it's important to continuously invest in it. We certainly do. We are active members of the Couples Ministry at our church and I am also an active member of the Wives Support Ministry. Through these ministries, we receive and participate in year-round education on the necessary skills to be a good spouse and to move your marriage forward always.

Now this topic, Trust, is very dear to me. I want to share with you that Derrick and I dealt with infidelity and it rocked us. I was pregnant with our first child at the time and the stress of that breach in trust was overwhelming. I didn't know what to do, how to handle it, or how to move forward. I couldn't even stand to look at him. The pain, hurt, and disappointment I felt was too large. There was a time when I didn't think I could move forward with him. Eventually, we got to a place where we were okay, we were moving forward, but our relationship didn't thrive. And that was essential to me, to us. So we had to figure this trust thing out and that what's we did. And I'm going to share exactly how I did that, how *we* did that together, in this book. I know our system works because it worked for us. I can happily say that I once again fully trust my husband. Let me say that again. I now fully trust my husband. And it feels incredible to be able to say that. It didn't happen overnight, but I put in the necessary work, Derrick did his part, and we now have a marriage that frankly rocks!

Rebuilding trust in your marriage or relationship will take both of you. You can't do it alone and you can't do it if your spouse or significant other is unwilling to do his or her part. The journey is different for each spouse. Based on my experience, both individually and as a coach, the spouse that was violated (the recipient of the breach) typically is most affected. I'm not diminishing the impact the breach has on the other spouse, because make no mistake, the consequences of that choice to commit the "act" will affect that spouse tremendously. The Principles and implementing steps outlined in this workbook will focus heavily on the steps the violated spouse should take to trust again, but will cover key things the spouse causing the breach must do to help his or her spouse, and rebuild trust. So with that, let's get started.

PRINCIPLE ONE: DO YOU WANT YOUR MARRIAGE?

Principle One requires an answer to this question, Do You Want Your Marriage? Let me repeat it, "Do You Want Your Marriage?" The answer to this question really sets the foundation for you to move forward. Based on my experience as a marriage coach, many couples are at this stage and are grappling with this precise question. Some of you reading this book may be thinking, of course I want my marriage. That's why I purchased this book. But let's dig a little deeper. Many express that they want their marriage after a significant breach in trust, but need their spouse to rebuild their trust before they can really commit to staying in the marriage, or need to first understand what happened and why their husband or wife cheated, spent all their money, kept secret accounts, whatever the breach in trust is, before they can really move forward. If that's you, then you too are at this threshold stage. Wanting your marriage means no conditions are attached. There is no, I want my marriage if x, y, and z happens. There is no, I want my marriage so long as my husband or wife does x, y, and z. There is no, I want my marriage because of my circumstances. So how do you figure this out, with all the emotions swirling around in your body? How do you figure this out with the Great Wall of China around your heart? This is how we tackled this first principle in our process.

When I found out Derrick cheated on me, I was devastated. I felt angry, disappointed, betrayed, hurt, and scared. I couldn't believe it. I thought things were great between us. And we had a baby on the way. It was one of the happiest times in my life. My first reaction was this is O V E R. I was so furious with him. The walls around my heart were made of titanium steel. Nothing was getting through them. I was in survival mode and that meant I needed him gone, out of my sight. We were having a baby, yes, but I was prepared to raise her solo. I didn't even want him around her. What lessons could he teach? I would figure out a way to take care of our daughter alone. And honestly, that's where I was for some time.

Derrick apologized profusely, asked for my forgiveness innumerable times, told me he made a mistake, told me he didn't care about *her*, said he never meant to hurt me, told me that he loved me more than anything, said he'd do anything to get *us* back, and on and on and on. I didn't want to hear any of it. I mean who cheats on the person you claim is your soul mate? Who cheats on the person you claim you want to spend the rest of your life with? Who cheats on the person you claim you can't imagine living without? Well he did. I listened and like many of you reading this book, I needed to understand why he cheated. I needed to know if it was me, was it something that I did, did I not satisfy his sexual needs? What happened?

During this period, Derrick too was distraught. He shared how disappointed and angry he was with himself. He shared, and I could actually see, how much pain he was in because he hurt and betrayed me. He repeatedly asked for forgiveness and showed true remorse. He "pulled out all the stops" as they say to try to win me back. As important as all that was, it didn't help much. My feelings were too raw, the hurt and anger profound. I was not sympathetic to his feelings. As the weeks passed, the overwhelming anger subsided and I was able to think without my feelings and emotions completely running the show. I began to open my heart a little. I was still head-over-heels in love and even with this breach in trust, I could not imagine life without him. I couldn't imagine raising my daughter without him. He promised never to do it again and to do whatever I asked him to do. So I agreed to give us another chance and move forward. Some of you reading this book are right where I was. You've made a decision to move forward. But, you really haven't answered the question. Do you WANT your marriage? Let's discuss what that really means, this concept of wanting and choosing your marriage.

My initial decision to move forward in my relationship was conditional. It was based primarily on my circumstances, as we were expecting a child, and he committed never to cheat again. We moved forward and as time went on, things got better. He was a boy scout. He attended to my every need. He gave me space when I needed it and managed to handle my yo-yo emotions. I was feeling better and had warmed to him quite a bit, but I wasn't all in. I couldn't take down those walls. I was always wondering what he was up to, and questioning his whereabouts. I'd check his phone and email periodically, looking for *stuff.* Anytime something remotely related to cheating came up on the television or elsewhere, I was right back to where I was when I discovered he cheated. We'd have arguments about it and I'd withdraw and be distant.

This didn't happen every day of course, but it happened and I hated it. It was a vicious cycle. I didn't want to live this way, not really trusting him. If we were going to be together forever, I had to do something different.

So I started journaling. I asked myself, why did I want to be with him, and I made myself answer this question without considering that we were having a child. I answered this question without considering the opinions of my family and friends. I answered this question without considering that he promised never to cheat again. And I got specific. I wrote down that I loved his sense of humor and how he made me laugh like none other. I wrote down that he totally gets me and doesn't try to change me. With him, I can be 100% me, flaws and all, without fear that he'd leave me—something I'd never experienced before in a relationship. I wrote down that he listens to me and really values my opinion. I wrote down that he treats me like his equal and partner and that he strives to think about us first before himself, something I truly appreciated.

I asked myself, did I really want this man who'd broken my heart to be there with me, at my side, through all the other storms that I would face during this journey called life. Did I want him there when my parents or other loved ones died? Did I want him there when I got my next big promotion? I asked myself did I want him to be my confidant. Is he the one that I wanted to share my most intimate thoughts with, a funny story with, the one that I want to experience life with? Is he still that one?

Answering these questions helped me to really crystallize what I wanted for me, Davida. Answering these questions helped me see clearly that I still wanted him and I wanted us. That want and desire was not based on what he needed to do to fix things. It was not based on the fact that we were having a baby. It was not based on what my friends and family would think. It was not based on what he promised to do or not to do. It was based on what I wanted and saw for myself for the rest of my life. That's really what WANTING your marriage is all about.

As for Derrick, he too took a hard look at what he wanted. Remember, you both have to want your marriage. Derrick had to consider if he was truly sorry for his indiscretion. He didn't want to hurt me, but was he sorry because he viewed his decision as a personal failure or because he hurt me. Derrick loved me, yes, but he had to consider if he really wanted to be married, and if so, to me. He had to consider if he was willing to change his behavior. Derrick spent hours considering these questions. Ultimately, he too concluded that he wanted us.

Steps to Implement Principle One

With this principle in mind, it's important for you and your spouse to answer the question, Do You Want Your Marriage? The following exercises are designed to help you do just that.

Exercise 1 (non-breaching *spouse*)

Answer the following questions:

1. Why do you want to be with your spouse? Be very specific. Focus on the qualities and characteristics your spouse possesses. What contributions does he or she make to your life?

   _____

   _____

   _____

   _____

   _____

   _____

   _____

   _____

   _____

2. Why don't you want to be with your spouse? Be very specific. What qualities or characteristics of your spouse are problematic? Do not focus on the breach itself.

_____

_____

_____

_____

_____

_____

_____

_____

_____

_____

_____

_____

_____

_____

_____

_____

_____

_____

3. Do you want your spouse above all to be with you during the challenges you will face in your life? Why or why not and explain in detail.

_____

_____

_____

_____

_____

_____

_____

_____

_____

_____

_____

_____

_____

_____

_____

4. Do you want your spouse to be your confidant? Why or why not? Explain.

_____

_____

_____

_____

_____

_____

_____

_____

_____

_____

_____

_____

_____

_____

_____

_____

5. Do you want to continue being married to your spouse? Why? Explain in detail.

_____

_____

_____

_____

_____

_____

_____

_____

_____

_____

_____

_____

_____

_____

_____

_____

_____

Exercise 2 (breaching spouse)

If you're the breaching spouse, answer the following questions.

1. Are you truly sorry for what you did and why? As part of your response, address whether you are sorry primarily because you hurt/disappointed your spouse?

   _____

   _____

   _____

   _____

   _____

   _____

   _____

   _____

   _____

   _____

   _____

   _____

   _____

   _____

   _____

2. How do you view the "act" you committed? Do you see it as a personal failure? Explain in detail.

_____

_____

_____

_____

_____

_____

_____

_____

_____

_____

_____

_____

_____

_____

_____

_____

_____

DAVIDA GRANT BROWN

3. Do you believe a change in your behavior is required? Explain why or why not?

_____

_____

_____

_____

_____

_____

_____

_____

_____

_____

_____

_____

_____

_____

_____

_____

_____

_____

_____

24

4. Do you want to be married to your spouse? Why?

_____

_____

_____

_____

_____

_____

_____

_____

_____

_____

_____

_____

_____

_____

_____

_____

_____

_____

Exercise 3

Review your answers to Exercises 1 and 2 together and discuss.

This may be a difficult discussion, but you both need to hear the answers to these questions. You both ultimately need to figure out together if you WANT your marriage. And if you both decide you want your marriage, you are ready for Principle Two.

PRINCIPLE TWO: THE RIGHT MINDSET

Principle Two is all about the having right mindset for marriage. This step in many ways requires you to go back to the drawing board. If you've been dealing with a significant breach in trust, you've been off kilter. You have not been focused on moving your marriage forward, being the best spouse you can be, or believing in your spouse. You haven't been living up to your capacity as a spouse because you've been mired in all the anger, hurt, and frustration you've suffered due to the breach in trust. But now that you've decided that you WANT your marriage, you need a mental reset. You need to mentally do what it takes so that you're in a position to be the best possible spouse you can be *and to be that spouse* REQUIRES that you trust your spouse.

Before we get into reconditioning your mind to trust again, let me explain what I mean by having the right mindset for marriage. It's important that you understand this concept because you can't trust again if you lack the right mindset for marriage. Having the right mindset for marriage means believing and understanding that you have the capacity to be a great spouse. This may sound intuitive or even easy, but it's not. So often, our minds are full of can'ts or won'ts in a relationship. I can't give in here or there. I won't do this or that...I can't get over what he or she did, I can't trust him or her because I've been hurt, I won't do this or that, until he or she does... All of these can'ts and won'ts undermine your ability to be a great spouse. Marriage can be challenging. You and your spouse will not always agree. You and your spouse will hurt and disappoint each other during the journey. But none of that should be a permanent barrier to your ability to move forward together. Moving forward together always includes putting your best forward and doing and being the best spouse you can be.

After a major breach in trust, you rightfully may question whether you can trust again, which in essence questions whether you have the capacity to be a great spouse. Understand, you cannot be a GREAT spouse if you do not trust your spouse. Distrust equates to walls around your heart and that will be a barrier to you living up to your potential as a spouse. So, you may be wondering, after all that's happened, whether you have the capacity to be a great spouse. The answer is a resounding, YES. It's in your DNA. Each of us are born of God, so that means we have the capacity to do all things. The Bible speaks directly to this ability. Genesis 1:27 states,

> So God created mankind **in his** own **image**, **in** the **image** of God he created them; male and female he created them.

This means we are a reflection of God and because we are, we are capable of doing all things because God can do all things. Philippians 4:13 and Matthew 17:20 state, respectively,

"I **can do all** this through him who gives me strength."

"Because you have so little faith. Truly I tell you, if you have faith as small as a **mustard seed**, you can say to this mountain, 'Move from here to there,' and it will move. Nothing will be impossible for you."

These two passages make clear that there is nothing too big for you because God has given you the innate ability to handle it and move forward.

God created marriage to reflect his love. So of course he's given each of us the innate tools we need to be the very best spouse. Having this capacity for greatness doesn't mean perfection, but it means that you have the innate capability to excel in marriage, even after a tremendous failure in the marriage. You need only tap into your God-given skills.

Having the right mindset also requires an understanding and acceptance of what a great marriage requires: commitment, consistency, sacrifice, and accountability. All great marriages have these. There's no way around it. Let's explore these components further.

     o   *Commitment*

Are you committed to stick it out, no matter what? You answered yes to the question, Do You Want Your Marriage?, so it's quite possible that you have this component covered. Importantly, it's critical that you understand that the problem you're facing won't be the last valley you experience in your marriage. Commitment in marriage is not problem-specific. It applies, regardless of the problem. So when I ask are you committed to stick it out, I'm asking whether you are willing to stay and work it out during the good, the bad, *and the ugly* of marriage? I often ask my clients to imagine the three worst things their spouse could do. And I mean the worst. Yep, I'm talking about things like repeated infidelity (perhaps with someone you know), complete financial ruin (you're practically on the street), the loss of a child or loved one due your spouse's negligence, mistake, or actions, or perhaps physical/emotional abuse. Harsh, right? But this is reality. Many couples face these and other life-altering situations during the course of marriage. During those times, would you be willing to work through it with your spouse (of course assuming your spouse is also willing), and in so doing, give everything you've got to push past it? That's commitment folks. It's understanding that mistakes—and some big ones—may happen during the journey, and having the mindset to dig your heels in and fight through it. No problem is bigger than your marriage. The only question is whether, when faced with that problem, you have a mindset of commitment to work through and ultimately resolve it. Couples with *great* marriages that last a lifetime do just that.

    o   *Consistency*

You have to mentally embrace the fact that it takes daily effort to have a successful marriage. That's consistency. It requires continuous investment in the marriage, *even when things are great*. I often tell my clients to treat your marriage like you do your body. Feed it every day. Nourishment can take so many forms: quality time, honoring and fulfilling the commitments you've made to your spouse, attending marriage-enrichment seminars and workshops. When you invest in your marriage during the good times, that nourishment sustains you during the bad and ugly times of marriage.

Consistency is also required when you are in a valley in your marriage. So, for example, let's say you and your spouse are at an impasse on a particular issue and neither of you are particularly happy with the other. During this period, you still have to do all the things required for your marriage. You must continue to communicate. The silent treatment or cold shoulder must never be an option. You still have to have sex with your spouse. Many spouses, particularly wives, refuse to have sex with their husbands when there is conflict in the marriage. Refusing to have sex because you're mad is selfish and contrary to the will of God. The Bible, in fact, is very clear on this point.

1 Corinthians 7:2-5 "But because of the temptation to sexual immorality, each man should have his own wife and each woman her own husband. The husband should give to his wife her conjugal rights, and likewise the wife to her husband. For the wife does not have authority over her own body, but the husband does. Likewise the husband does not have authority over his own body, but the wife does. Do not deprive one another, except perhaps by agreement for a limited time, that you may devote yourselves to prayer; but then come together again, so that Satan may not tempt you because of your lack of self-control.

You also have to continue to make quality time for your spouse and perform the day-to-day tasks you committed to, refusing to let them slip until "you make up." In essence, consistency requires that you continuously honor your spouse and marriage daily.

o   *Sacrifice*

You have to compromise and often put your spouse's needs and desires first to move your marriage forward. That's sacrifice. This is a big one for many couples, especially when one spouse vehemently disagrees with his or her spouse's position in a certain area. But the fact is, you won't always get your way, and neither will your spouse. Compromise is required over and over again to move your marriage forward. In fact, sometimes, you have to fully give in to your spouse's position (complete sacrifice) to move the matter forward. As the saying goes, you have to learn to pick your battles.

Notwithstanding the foregoing, sacrifice does not include departing from your core values, which should be based on God's word. If you and your spouse are at an impasse, compromise and sacrifice require that you seek God's counsel.

Philippians 4:6 Do not be anxious about anything, but in everything by prayer and supplication with thanksgiving let your requests be made known to God.

The point here is you must understand that during your marriage, you will have to make concessions in order to move the marriage forward. Understanding this reality is key to a great marriage.

    o   *Accountability*

You and your spouse have to take ownership of your actions. That's accountability. The blame game has no place in marriage. I know it sounds intuitive, but it is so easy to pass the buck when something goes awry. In marriage, you and your spouse have to do what you say you're going to do and accept the consequences when you fail to do so. This necessarily requires that you and your spouse understand your individual roles in the marriage and establish specific responsibilities/tasks/etc. for the marriage to work.

When you mentally believe that you have the capacity to be a great spouse and recognize and accept what's required of you in your marriage, you consequently will embrace the decision to trust your spouse. That's because, you can't be the spouse you need to be and do all the things marriage requires without trust. You've already made the decision that you want your marriage. So really embracing this notion of having the right mindset for marriage will put you in position to make the decision to trust again.

It is so critically important that you understand that trusting your spouse is a *choice* you make. Your spouse does not create the trust. You choose to give it.

Now getting your mindset back on track so that you can make the decision to trust can take some work. After experiencing a major breach, those pesky emotions are likely still there and your skepticism likely remains. That's completely natural. Trusting is a process. But there are concrete things that you can do to help reset your mindset so you're in a position to trust again. Let me share how we implemented this principle.

First, every day I told myself, and spoke out loud, that I trust Derrick. I stopped saying, I'm going to try to trust you or that I'm working on trusting you, or things of that nature. I stated it as if it were so. That's part of the mental re-conditioning. I needed to think it and hear it in order to begin to believe that I actually had the capacity to trust him again.

Second, I frequently told Derrick, I trust you, as if it were so. Now Derrick knows me like the back of his hand, so he knew I didn't fully trust him yet. But he understood that I was going through a process. He understood that I was making the mental decisions and changes that were necessary to *allow* me to *believe* that I could trust him.

During this stage in the process, I had many challenging days. I'd see things or hear things that made me think about the breach in trust and at times my emotions would flood me. I willed myself and forced myself to push past them. Sometimes it was a herculean effort, but I stayed the course. I'd go back to the journaling I talked about in Principle One, which helped me decide that yes, I want my marriage. I'd also challenge myself to answer, Is this issue of trust bigger than my marriage? Every time my answer was no. Is this issue something that I am going to allow to defeat me, if you will, and keep me in a place that I did not want to be, which was second guessing him? Every time my answer was no. Would I allow the emotions that were a by-product of the breach in trust rob me of

what I wanted most, which was to be happily
married to Derrick? My answer every time was no.

Third, I read detailed testimonies from
other couples who faced infidelity and overcame it.
And there are so many out there. As a wife, I was
particularly drawn to the stories of other wives and
how they worked through the issue of infidelity and
made the choice to trust again. Obviously, every
situation is different, but there is extreme value in
seeing or knowing that another person that's felt the
hurt, anger, pain, frustration, and embarrassment
that you feel was able to get through it and move
forward with their spouse. I flooded my mind with
these stories. Some I read seemingly a million
times. They emboldened me and gave me a
tremendous form of support and encouragement
because I felt like it was attainable. They helped
confirm for me that it was possible to *make a choice*
to trust again after infidelity and actually do it.

Fourth, I did what I call the great purge. I
removed any and everything that was contrary to

my goal of changing my mindset and trusting again. That meant I had to cut some people out of my life during this period of time, including family. Some of them knew what was going on and I knew I was not mentally strong enough to handle any negative comments or vibes. I needed to surround myself solely with people who were supportive and encouraging, so that's what I did. It's important to be extremely careful with who has your ear. It's easy to be influenced when you are in a vulnerable state. In fact, I stopped discussing the matter with outsiders. This was hard at first because I wanted the support. But at the end of the day, I had to go through this journey. Once I made the decision that I wanted to be with Derrick, I had to set things in motion to accomplish that and outsiders just weren't able to help me or us. I also stopped watching television shows that were counter to my goal. So many deal with the issue of cheating and most aren't helpful. This purging helped to keep me focused on the end goal, which again, in this step was changing my mindset.

Last and certainly not least, throughout this process I read my bible and prayed. If you are a believer, you know that God's word addresses every issue under the sun. I focused on the scriptures that spoke to my capacity to do all things, scriptures that spoke to the fact that we are all born of His seed, meaning that I have the ability to conquer any challenge before me because it's in my DNA.

When I prayed, I asked God to help me change my mindset so I could move forward in my relationship. I prayed that He give me the ability to get back on track to being the best wife I could be, to being a trusting wife. I prayed and believed that with His help, I could make the decision to trust and be confident in my ability to do so.

During this phase of the process, Derrick too had to reset his mind. He had to believe that he could be a faithful spouse. He had to believe that he was trustworthy. He had to accept his tremendous failure, particularly as head of our household and my protector. In many ways, he had to believe in me and in us. He had to believe that I could one day look at him the same way. He had to believe that he could help us get back to that place. He had to believe that he had the wherewithal to endure my yo-yo emotions, my physical and emotional withdrawal, and all the other consequences of the breach.

Truly making the decision to trust Derrick didn't happen overnight, but as I worked through the steps I just described, I reached a place where I was mentally ready to trust him. Derrick too realized that he was worthy of trust and that he had the ability to be a faithful spouse.

Steps to Implement Principle Two

Complete the following exercises, which are designed to enable you to reset your mind.

Exercise 1

For Principle One, you answered, Do You Want Your Marriage? Now that you've answered yes to that question, I want you to answer the following questions:

(1) What does having a thriving marriage mean to you? (both)

_____

_____

_____

_____

_____

_____

_____

_____

_____

_____

_____

_____

_____

(2) Do you want a thriving marriage? Why?
Are you ready to commit to doing what it
takes to be the best spouse you can be, living
up to your capacity. (both)

_____

_____

_____

_____

_____

_____

_____

_____

_____

_____

_____

_____

_____

_____

_____

_____

_____

(3) Do you believe you have the capacity to fully trust again? Why or why not? Explain in detail. (non-breaching spouse)

_____

_____

_____

_____

_____

_____

_____

_____

_____

_____

_____

_____

_____

_____

_____

_____

_____

_____

(4) If you don't think you have the capacity to fully trust again, why? Why is it impossible to trust again? (non-breaching spouse)

_____

_____

_____

_____

_____

_____

_____

_____

_____

_____

_____

_____

_____

_____

_____

_____

_____

(5) Do you believe you are trustworthy? Why?
Explain in detail. (breaching spouse)

_____

_____

_____

_____

_____

_____

_____

_____

_____

_____

_____

_____

_____

_____

_____

_____

(6) Do you understand that the "breach" was a failure on your part? Why was it a failure? (breaching spouse)

_____

_____

_____

_____

_____

_____

_____

_____

_____

_____

_____

_____

_____

_____

_____

_____

_____

_____

(7) Do you believe you have the capacity to refrain from committing that breach again? Why or why not? (breaching spouse)

_____

_____

_____

_____

_____

_____

_____

_____

_____

_____

_____

_____

_____

_____

_____

_____

_____

_____

(8) Is the breach in trust bigger than your
   marriage? (both)

_____

_____

_____

_____

_____

_____

_____

_____

_____

_____

_____

_____

_____

_____

_____

_____

_____

When you finish answering these questions, discuss them together. This will give you a window into each other's mental thoughts and processes. Share your thoughts on each other's responses and be open to each other's comments. Remember, together, you've already made the decision that you want your marriage. Everything that follows is a step towards rebuilding the trust in the marriage. It's critically important that you are on the same page and are completely transparent with each other to move the process forward.

Exercise 2 (non-breaching spouse)

Every day, state in the affirmative, I trust my husband or wife. Say it out loud with gusto. This helps feed your mind with positivity and conditions it to trust again.

Exercise 3 (breaching spouse)

Every day, state out loud, I am trustworthy. Again, you're conditioning your mind.

Exercise 4 (both)

Perform a purge. List everything and everyone in your life that will or potentially could derail you in making the choice to trust your spouse or prevent you from being trustworthy.

_____

_____

_____

_____

_____

_____

_____

_____

_____

_____

_____

_____

_____

_____

_____

_____

_____

_____

_____

_____

_____

_____

_____

_____

_____

_____

_____

_____

_____

_____

_____

_____

Discuss this list together and get rid of them.

Exercise 5 (both)

Find positive testimonies from other couples that experienced the specific breach in trust you are experiencing, made the choice to trust again, and rebuilt trust in their marriage. Read and reread and discuss together. Allow their stories to encourage you.

I believe if you work through these questions and take these actions, you'll have the right mindset to trust again.

PRINCIPLE THREE: FORGIVENESS

Principle Three is forgiveness. There is no way around this principle if you want to fully trust again. Forgiveness is a process. Let's be honest— it's unnatural and it can be very difficult to do. Like trust, forgiveness is something that you choose to do, and it's a daily choice. It also, in my opinion, has a mental and what I call a "heart" component, with both being equal in importance. When you make the mental choice to forgive, forgiveness is not complete. It's complete when your heart is free from the anger, hurt, and bitterness that has frankly held you hostage. And that takes time and it's perfectly okay.

Now for some of you, the process of forgiveness may start contemporaneously with or, in some instances, before the previous two principles. That too is perfectly okay. Forgiveness was the third step in my process because I knew I had to forgive Derrick for my own sanity, whether we stayed together or not. Knowing that, I concentrated my initial efforts on making the decision to stay in the relationship and then reconditioning my mind to trust again. With those two under my belt, I could fully focus on forgiveness and the remaining principle, which I'll cover in the next chapter. No matter the order, forgiveness is a must.

I suspect you've had to forgive in the past. Forgiveness is forgiveness and this breach in trust that you're dealing with doesn't require a different process to forgive. I'm often asked, how did I translate my *choice* to forgive Derrick to *actually* forgiving him in my heart? Here's what I did.

First and foremost, as I shared in Principle Two, I am a believer in God so I turned to Him for help. The Bible discusses the topic of forgiveness extensively. God unquestionably directs us to forgive and in fact commands us to do so. So many of the biblical verses have this concept of forgiving others the same way that God forgives you.

There was one verse in particular that stood out to me, Colossians 3:13, which says, "Bear with each other and forgive one another if any of you has a grievance against someone. Forgive as the Lord forgave you (NIV). This verse was right on point and spoke directly to what I was grappling with in trying to forgive Derrick. I meditated and reflected on those words over and over. I had a duty to forgive Derrick the way that God has forgiven, forgives, and will forgive me for the countless sins I've committed and will do. Once I made the *decision* to forgive him, I turned it over to God and asked that He help me with the second part, which was forgiving Derrick in my heart.

I do not believe that you can mentally decide to forgive and do nothing else but wait for "healing" in your heart. You have to do things to foster forgiveness. That's part of what I mean when I say that choosing to forgive is a daily choice. Here's what I did to foster forgiveness.

First, I made a detailed list of all the things I'd done over the years for which I sought forgiveness. This was not limited to things I'd done to Derrick, but others in my life as well. And I mean I wrote them down. Of course I couldn't remember everything, but my list was long. Some didn't seem to be "major" things, but they were things that I did that hurt, upset, or even betrayed others. And I wanted their forgiveness. Some of them were "BIG" things, things that cost me friendships. This exercise helped me to see that I too need forgiveness for things that I do, that I too want fervently to be forgiven by my family and friends for those deeds. Derrick was seeking the same.

Second, I spent lots and lots of one-on-one quality time with Derrick. After the affair, I withdrew quite a bit and didn't want to be around him much. I still loved him, but the hurt and disappointment was front and center. But when you spend time with someone you care about, you care even more, *and that caring affects your heart*. That increase in caring and love starts to chip away at the hurt, helping you with forgiveness. We spent time doing the things that we absolutely love doing together, allowing us to really reconnect. Things were shaky at first because I was so hurt and pissed, but the more time we spent together with consistency, that wall around my heart started to tumble down. I could so clearly see all the things I love about him. I could see all the day-to-day things he does for me, showing that he is in fact trustworthy. That made me care more and more and allowed forgiveness to really take root in my heart. So in a nutshell, mentally choosing to forgive him, relying on my faith in God that I could do it and trusting that He'd help change my heart, and spending an insane amount of one-on-one time with

Derrick enabled me *over time* to forgive him. The hurt and anger is no longer in my heart. That's how I know that I've truly forgiven Derrick for this breach in trust.

As for exercises for this step, as I've shared, you should already have a process in place for forgiveness. Use that process here. If you need help with making the choice to forgive or translating that decision into forgiveness in your heart, the following exercises should help you.

Steps to Implement Principle Three

Exercise 1 (both)

Read and meditate together on biblical scriptures on forgiveness. Below, I've provided a sampling of scriptures on forgiveness.

Ephesians 4:32 - And be ye kind one to another, tenderhearted, forgiving one another, even as God for Christ's sake hath forgiven you.

Mark 11:25 - And when ye stand praying, forgive, if ye have ought against any: that your Father also which is in heaven may forgive you your trespasses.

1 John 1:9 - If we confess our sins, he is faithful and just to forgive us [our] sins, and to cleanse us from all unrighteousness.

Matthew 6:15 - But if ye forgive not men their trespasses, neither will your Father forgive your trespasses.

<u>Matthew 18:21-22</u> - Then came Peter to him, and said, Lord, how oft shall my brother sin against me, and I forgive him? till seven times? Jesus saith unto him, I say not unto thee, Until seven times: but, Until seventy times seven.

<u>Matthew 6:14-15</u> - For if ye forgive men their trespasses, your heavenly Father will also forgive you: But if ye forgive not men their trespasses, neither will your Father forgive your trespasses.

<u>James 5:16</u> - Confess [your] faults one to another, and pray one for another, that ye may be healed. The effectual fervent prayer of a righteous man availeth much.

<u>Luke 6:27</u> - But I say unto you which hear, Love your enemies, do good to them which hate you.

<u>Colossians 3:13</u> - Forbearing one another, and forgiving one another, if any man have a quarrel against any: even as Christ forgave you, so also [do] ye.

1 Corinthians 10:13 - There hath no temptation taken you but such as is common to man: but God [is] faithful, who will not suffer you to be tempted above that ye are able; but will with the temptation also make a way to escape, that ye may be able to bear [it].

Luke 6:37 - Judge not, and ye shall not be judged: condemn not, and ye shall not be condemned: forgive, and ye shall be forgiven.

Romans 3:23 - For all have sinned, and come short of the glory of God.

Exercise 2 (both)

Read biblical accounts where individuals demonstrated forgiveness for seemingly extraordinary grievances.

<u>Two Great Examples</u>:

- *Joseph Forgives His Brothers* - The story of Joseph immediately comes to mind when I think about forgiveness. His brothers wanted to kill him because they were jealous of Joseph. Joseph was his dad's favorite and he had a unique gift—interpreting dreams. Joseph shared with his brothers that he had a dream that one day, they would bow before him. His brothers ultimately sold him into slavery and Joseph found himself in a number of precarious situations as a result, even prison. But eventually, because of his gift, Joseph was elevated to the second highest position in Egypt and during a famine, circumstances led his brothers to him, as they needed assistance. Ultimately, Joseph forgave them, embraced them, and moved forward with a relationship with them. There are many more details, but it's a powerful story (Genesis 37-50).

• *The Prodigal Son* – In this story, the father forgives his son for foolishly spending his inheritance. Specifically, the son asked his father for his portion of his inheritance, left his father's house with the money, and, once on his own, engaged in all sorts of debauchery. Eventually, the money ran out. He had no job, no food, and no friends. The son reasoned that it would be better to be a servant in his father's home than continuing to live as he was. So he decided to return to his father's home, hoping his father would allow him to be a servant. Upon his return, his father embraced him, forgiving him fully for his deeds (Luke 15).

The Bible is full of stories of forgiveness. Read
them together. Then, write down the lessons
learned from these stories and discuss together. It's
important that you encourage each other during this
process of forgiveness.

_____

_____

_____

_____

_____

_____

_____

_____

_____

_____

_____

_____

_____

_____

_____

_____

_____

_____

_____

_____

_____

_____

_____

_____

_____

_____

_____

_____

Exercise 3 (both)

Pray together daily. Ask God to step in and help change your heart. Ask God to help you be a supportive and patient spouse.

Exercise 4

Write down all the things you've done to your
spouse, wherein you've sought forgiveness. It may
not have been a major thing, but if it caused hurt or
pain, he or she has to forgive you. Do the same for
other key relationships. Take your time with this
exercise.

_____

_____

_____

_____

_____

_____

_____

_____

_____

_____

_____

_____

_____

_____

_____

_____

_____

_____

_____

_____

_____

_____

_____

_____

_____

_____

_____

_____

_____

_____

_____

Once you've finished, reflect on how you too need forgiveness in your relationships.

Exercise 5

Make the time for extensive one-on-one time with your spouse. Even if it feels forced, do it.

If this disconnect has been there for some time due to the breach in trust, you may be at a loss for what to do. To assist you, each of you should write down 10 activities you'd like to do together.

_____

_____

_____

_____

_____

_____

_____

_____

_____

_____

_____

_____

_____

_____

_____

During this time, don't focus on the trust issues or other issues plaguing your marriage. Focus on enjoying each other. Focus on the things you love about each other.

Exercise 6

Establish a daily activity that you commit to doing every day together (duration at least 15 minutes). To assist you here, each of you should individually list 5 things you could do daily together. Then compare and together choose an activity from the list. Endeavor to do this activity *every day*. Here are some suggestions to get you started.

Breakfast

Coffee/tea run

Workout

Cook a meal

A walk together

Shower together

Get dressed for work

Talking during work commute

List others

_____

_____

_____

_____

_____

_____

_____

_____

_____

Over time, you'll start to see your spouse with fresh eyes, allowing the process of forgiveness to complete.

PRINCIPLE FOUR: EXERCISING TRUST

This last principle, Exercising Trust, is a big one. Now that you've decided that you want your marriage, now that you've reset your mind to trust again, now that you're in the process of forgiving, it's time to act. Now, you have to actually *exercise* the trust.

Your spouse has to be an integral part of Principle Four. Before you can begin exercising trust, you and your spouse must really have a heart-to-heart about what happened. By this point, you've probably had a million conversations about it, but what I'm talking about is really figuring out what led to the breach. Most often, the "act" itself is just a symptom of underlying issues; such as poor communication, poor conflict resolution skills, and lack of intimacy. Your emotions hopefully are under control by now. You and your spouse must be at a point where you can talk about the underlying issues and what the two of you can do *together* as a *team* to correct and resolve those issues. While your spouse is 100% at fault for committing the "breach" in question, understand that if there are underlying issues in your marriage—and most often there are—you have a part in that. The underlying issue is not all your spouse's fault. It is crucial that you, the violated spouse, understand and accept this before moving forward.

It may take you some time to fully digest what I just said. Often, when there's a major breach in trust, the violated spouse is not willing to own up to other issues in the marriage. That is key. If you need help in figuring out if you have any underlying issues, don't be afraid to seek help. Counseling or coaching may be in your best interest to help you really crystallize what the gaps are in your marriage. If you don't, the issue is more likely than not to repeat itself.

Importantly, it's not enough to just figure out what the issues are in your marriage. In my experience, most couples know what their issues are. Despite that knowledge, many don't take action to fix them, leaving gaping holes in their marriage. If you truly want to move forward in your marriage and fully trust again, you have to implement steps to fix your issues. Doing so will give you both confidence that your marriage is on track and that you can in fact have a successful marriage full of trust.

Now, as I stated in Principle Two, your spouse can't rebuild your trust. Trusting is a choice. That said, your spouse absolutely can and must help you in that journey. And, you must do your part too, meaning you must avail yourself of opportunities to actually exercise trusting your spouse. So, in addition to figuring out if you have

any underlying issues in your marriage, and if so,
implementing specific steps to fix them, as part of
this process, the two of you need to set expectations
and goals for your marriage. Something went awry
before. So you can't keep doing whatever it was
that you were doing before. It certainly is *possible*
that you were doing your part and your spouse
wasn't. But with this step, the both of you need to
figure out what can and needs to be done to
minimize the likelihood of a repeat breach. And
really be honest about it. There have to be some
ground rules here. The expectations must be
attainable. You must refrain from asking him or her
to do something they can't do or can't do for the
long haul. You must refrain from requesting things
to punish your spouse. That's a recipe for failure.
You must also refrain from making changes or
setting expectations that don't allow *you* the ability
to exercise trust. Rebuilding trust for the violated
spouse is not a wait-and-see strategy. You aren't
waiting to see if your spouse can live up to the set
expectations. You too must act, and by act I mean

you must exercise trust during this process. So, let me share how we handled this.

Derrick and I had many lengthy heart-to-heart discussions about cheating and what led to his indiscretion. We determined that our communication skills were good, we were able to manage conflict well in our relationship, and we were intimately connected. One of the many things we discussed was temptations. Derrick admitted that he at times struggles with temptations involving women, particularly aggressive women and particularly when he's in an environment that facilitates and supports fulfillment of those temptations. Whoa did I hate hearing that. It really hurt my ego. But he was being honest, and we needed to tackle that together.

So we took a hard look at what he does, and the scenarios where he felt most tempted. One particular activity we identified involved his motorcycle club. That club had lots of activities with lots of single women, and based on what he shared, the women that attended his club's events are very aggressive. *Many are down for whatever.* Motorcycle club events aren't my cup of tea, AT ALL, so I rarely if ever attend events. As we thought through this, we had to consider whether he should continue being a member of that club.

I'll admit, my first reaction was, nope. That's done. No more motorcycle club for you. And I was at that place for months. But as I thought about this and we discussed it together, that was a drastic response AND it did not allow me the opportunity to exercise trust. While his club had events that were problematic, I ultimately had to realize that the club wasn't the issue, it was Derrick. Single women are everywhere. Derrick had to be able to manage his temptations, regardless of the environment. We both had to recognize and accept that.

So, first and foremost, Derrick agreed to get individual counseling. With help, he was able to work through and successfully manage temptations.

It's important to note that he continues to work on this issue. Counseling didn't make the issue go away. Derrick had to and has to make a conscious decision not to take advantage of those temptations when presented. His counselor helped him develop the tools he needed in order to do that.

Second, after many discussions, we decided together that Derrick would remain a member of his motorcycle club, but he would not attend nighttime or any party-type activities hosted by the club unless I attended, and his annual trips to Myrtle Beach for Bike Week were no more. This agreement enabled my husband to continue doing something he loved—riding bikes with the other members—while minimizing the likelihood that he'd be in unhealthy situations, like the parties and overnight trips. While Derrick was at a point where he was able to manage his temptations, Derrick understood and determined on his own that being in an environment that encouraged debauchery was not good for him or our marriage. For me, agreeing that he should stay a member in the club allowed me the opportunity to exercise trust. Derrick continued to periodically go on bike rides with his club and I had to trust that during those times, he was being faithful. There would be no drive bys, checking of his phone or email, or any of those things. I had to trust he was where he said he'd be, doing what he said. Once we reached this agreement, we committed to honor it and be accountable. And it's working.

So, as you think through what changes need to be made in your relationship, as you set expectations, make sure they are realistic, reasonable, and something that you both support.

Once you establish those expectations, you must be accountable. You must do what you've agreed upon. Point blank. Point blank. Any changes to those expectations or actions must not occur without consultation with your spouse. Point blank.

Now, things change over time and that's perfectly okay. If you want to revisit certain aspects of the expectations or goals you've set with your spouse, do it. The key is doing so *before* you make any changes thereto.

As you go through this process, transparency is key. The appearance of impropriety is unacceptable. If in doubt, don't do it unless and until you discuss the matter with your spouse. And each of you should have full access to each other and be fully in the loop as to what's going on with the other, particularly with respect to any activities related in any way to the breach.

Steps to Implement Principle Four

Exercise 1

The following exercises will help you identify any underlying issues in your marriage. Keep an open mind here as you perform these exercises. Your spouse may reveal some things you had no clue about. You may think you're communicating well and your spouse doesn't. You may think arguing and making up and arguing and making up is cool. Your spouse may not. You may think having sex once a week is enough. Your spouse may not. What I'm getting at here is that you need to discuss every major category that impacts your marriage to see if there are any issues therein that contributed to the breach. Communication, Conflict, Intimacy, and Finances are the big ones. Once you figure them out, implement a plan to address them. Consider counseling if your marriage is in crisis, meaning you are considering divorce or communication has effectively shut down. If you're not in crisis, coaching is appropriate. Implementing a plan to address the underlying issues is a must to fully rebuild trust.

Exercise 1a. Individually, define what each of the following terms means to you with respect to your marriage.

Effective Communication:

_____

_____

_____

_____

_____

_____

_____

_____

_____

Sex:

_____

_____

_____

_____

_____

_____

_____

_____

_____

Resolving or Managing Conflict:

_____

_____

_____

_____

_____

_____

_____

Financial Management:

_____

_____

_____

_____

_____

_____

_____

_____

Friendship:

_____

_____

_____

_____

_____

_____

_____

Emotional Intimacy:

_____

_____

_____

_____

_____

_____

_____

_____

_____

Spiritual Intimacy:

_____

_____

_____

_____

_____

_____

_____

_____

_____

Exercise 1(b) Individually rate on a scale of 1 to 5 (5 being the best) how your marriage fares in these areas. Circle the number:

Effective Communication

       1   2   3   4   5

Sex

       1   2   3   4   5

Resolving/Managing Conflict

       1   2   3   4   5

Financial Management

       1   2   3   4   5

Friendship

       1   2   3   4   5

Emotional Intimacy

       1   2   3   4   5

Spiritual Intimacy

    1   2   3   4   5

Then compare your answers. Really have heart-to-heart discussions about where you are in sync with your responses and where you aren't. You will have differences.

Exercise 1(c) For the areas where you differ, determine why you differ?

Effective Communication: We differ because

_____

_____

_____

_____

_____

_____

_____

_____

_____

Sex: We differ because

_____

_____

_____

_____

_____

_____

_____

_____

_____

Resolving/Managing Conflict: We differ because

_____

_____

_____

_____

_____

_____

_____

_____

_____

_____

_____

_____

Financial Management: We differ because

_____

_____

_____

_____

_____

_____

_____

_____

_____

_____

_____

Friendship: We differ because

_____

_____

_____

_____

_____

_____

_____

_____

_____

_____

_____

_____

_____

Emotional Intimacy: We differ because

_____

_____

_____

_____

_____

_____

_____

Spiritual Intimacy: We differ because

_____

_____

_____

_____

_____

Exercise 1(d) Using the knowledge you've gained from Exercises 1a-1c, particularly your new understanding of your differences, discuss and agree upon your goal for your marriage in each of these areas.

Effective Communication: Our goal in this area is to

_____

_____

_____

_____

_____

_____

_____

_____

_____

_____

_____

_____

_____

Sex: Our goal in this area is to

_____

_____

_____

_____

_____

_____

_____

_____

_____

_____

Resolving/Managing Conflict: Our goal in this area
is to

_____

_____

_____

_____

_____

_____

_____

_____

_____

_____

_____

_____

Financial Management: Our goal in this area is to

_____

_____

_____

_____

_____

_____

_____

_____

_____

_____

_____

_____

Friendship: Our goal in this area is to

_____

_____

_____

_____

_____

_____

_____

_____

_____

_____

Emotional Intimacy: Our goal in this area is to

_____

_____

_____

_____

_____

_____

_____

_____

_____

_____

_____

_____

Spiritual Intimacy: Our goal in this area is to

_____

_____

_____

_____

_____

_____

_____

_____

_____

_____

_____

_____

Exercise 1(e) Individually, detail the specific, individual steps you believe you and your spouse should take to help achieve the goals.

Effective Communication: To achieve our goal, I should

_____

_____

_____

_____

_____

_____

_____

_____

_____

My spouse should

_____

_____

_____

_____

_____

_____

_____

_____

_____

_____

Sex: To achieve our goal, I should

_____

_____

_____

_____

_____

_____

_____

_____

_____

_____

_____

_____

_____

My spouse should

_____

_____

_____

_____

_____

_____

_____

_____

_____

_____

_____

Resolving/Managing Conflict: To achieve our goal,
I should

_____

_____

_____

_____

_____

_____

_____

_____

_____

_____

_____

_____

_____

My spouse should

_____

_____

_____

_____

_____

_____

_____

_____

_____

_____

_____

_____

Financial Management: To achieve our goal, I should

_____

_____

_____

_____

_____

_____

_____

_____

_____

_____

My spouse should

_____

_____

_____

_____

_____

_____

_____

_____

_____

_____

_____

_____

Friendship: To achieve our goal, I should

_____

_____

_____

_____

_____

_____

_____

_____

_____

_____

_____

_____

_____

_____

My spouse should

_____

_____

_____

_____

_____

_____

_____

_____

_____

_____

_____

Emotional Intimacy: To achieve our goal, I should

_____

_____

_____

_____

_____

_____

_____

_____

_____

_____

My spouse should

_____

_____

_____

_____

_____

_____

_____

_____

_____

_____

_____

_____

Spiritual Intimacy: To achieve our goal, I should

_____

_____

_____

_____

_____

_____

_____

_____

_____

_____

My spouse should

_____

_____

_____

_____

_____

_____

_____

_____

_____

_____

_____

_____

Exercise 1(f) Review your answers to Exercise 1(e) together. Then agree upon the specific things you and your spouse *will do* to achieve each goal. Compromise will be required. Once agreed upon, you must commit to honor the agreement.

Effective Communication: To achieve our goal, I will

_____

_____

_____

_____

_____

_____

_____

My spouse will

_____

_____

_____

_____

_____

_____

_____
_____
_____
_____

Sex: To achieve our goal, I will

_____
_____
_____
_____
_____
_____
_____
_____
_____
_____
_____
_____

My spouse will

_____
_____

_____

_____

_____

_____

_____

_____

_____

_____

_____

Resolving/Managing Conflict: To achieve our goal,
I will

_____

_____

_____

_____

_____

_____

_____

_____

_____

_____

_____

My spouse will

_____

_____

_____

_____

_____

_____

_____

_____

_____

_____

_____

Financial Management: To achieve our goal, I will

_____

_____

_____

_____

_____

_____

_____

_____

_____

My spouse will

_____

_____

_____

_____

_____

_____

_____

_____

_____

_____

_____

_____

_____

Friendship: To achieve our goal, I will

_____

_____

_____

_____

_____

_____

_____

_____

_____

_____

_____

My spouse will

_____

_____

_____

_____

_____

_____

_____

_____

_____

_____

_____

Emotional Intimacy: To achieve our goal, I will

_____

_____

_____

_____

_____

_____

My spouse will

Spiritual Intimacy: To achieve our goal, I will

_____

_____

_____

_____

_____

_____

_____

_____

My spouse will

_____

_____

_____

_____

_____

_____

_____

_____

_____

Exercise 2

Set expectations for your marriage relating to the breach. Here, I'm referring to the Dos and Don'ts.

Exercise 2(a) What actions should you take (or abstain from) to minimize a reoccurrence of the "act". Be honest and don't sugarcoat it.

I should do the following:

_____

_____

_____

_____

_____

_____

_____

_____

_____

_____

_____

_____

_____

I should not do the following:

I expect my spouse to do the following:

_____

_____

_____

_____

_____

_____

_____

_____

_____

_____

I expect my spouse not to do the following:

_____

_____

_____

_____

_____

_____

_____

_____

_____

_____

_____

_____

Then review your individual responses together.
Take the time to really consider what your spouse
wants.

Exercise 2(b) Together, agree upon your expectations of each other.

I agree to do the following:

_____

_____

_____

_____

_____

_____

_____

_____

_____

I agree not to do the following:

_____

_____

_____

_____

_____

_____

_____

_____

_____

_____

My spouse agrees to do the following:

_____

_____

_____

_____

_____

_____

_____

_____

_____

_____

_____

_____

_____

My spouse agrees not to do the following:

_____

_____

_____

_____

_____

_____

_____

_____

_____

_____

_____

Exercise 3 (non-breaching spouse)

Together, identify opportunities to exercise trust. If the breach in trust dealt with finances, for example, what are some available opportunities that will allow your spouse to spend money in a responsible way and allow you to step back and trust that he or she is doing just that?

_____

_____

_____

_____

_____

_____

_____

_____

_____

_____

_____

_____

_____

_____

_____

_____

CONCLUSION

So those are our Four Principles to rebuilding trust in your marriage. As you can see, it takes work. Rebuilding trust won't happen overnight, but it can happen. Just stay the course. If you get stuck at a particular step, that's okay. Take a break, regroup, and try again. And if that doesn't work, get help. There are many qualified counseling and coaching services available to assist you in this area, including Marriage Rocks.

Good Luck!

ABOUT THE AUTHOR

Davida Grant Brown is the cofounder of Marriage Rocks, LLC. An ambassador for marriage, Davida launched www.yesmarriagerocks.com, an online platform that showcases happily married couples from around the world, and gives couples practical, proven tips and strategies for a marriage that will work, thrive, and last a lifetime. A practicing attorney, author, and certified marriage coach, Davida uses her skills to help couples identify issues or areas of concern in their marriage, implement a plan of action to address those issues, and measure the success of that plan through accountability metrics.

Davida is a highly sought after speaker on marriage-related issues. As the founder of Marriage Rocks, she has been featured on various media outlets, including WPGC, Urban Family Talk Radio, and Channel 8 News, Let's Talk Live DC.

CPSIA information can be obtained
at www.ICGtesting.com
Printed in the USA
FSOW02n0134160516
20487FS